REACH & TEACH
PRODUCT PROMOTION

Teaching Consumers To Buy

Lonny Kocina

REACH & TEACH Product Promotion
Teaching Consumers to Buy

First Printing: November 2007
Printed in the United States of America

Published by:
MID-AMERICA EVENTS & EXPOS, INC.®
350 W. Burnsville Parkway, Suite 350
Minneapolis, MN 55337

Phone: 800-999-4859 Fax: 612-798-7272
Email: media@mediarelations.com
Web page: www.publicity.com

Contents

By necessity this book is an overview of the marketing and promotional process. However, the primary purpose is to help you identify and use REACH & TEACH promotional channels. These channels give you the opportunity to deliver sales-rich content that will allow you to make a deeper connection with potential customers.

Chapter One

Putting Salesmanship Back in Your Marketing

Claude Hopkins, who wrote *My Life in Advertising* back in 1927, called advertising "salesmanship in print". There doesn't seem to be much salesmanship left in advertising today.

Marketing veered off course in the 70s and 80s when people reached an advertising saturation point. They could no longer absorb all of the ads that were being churned out so they stopped paying attention.

Advertising's answer to the dilemma was simple—be creative and do something that would shock consumers into watching. It was during this time that "creativity" and its close relative "humor" became a required component in the advertising formula. You could also say that advertising now served two masters with two different agendas. The old master was the product and its sales message, and the new master was the public and its demand to be entertained.

The advertising industry's response to the public's cry to be entertained spurred an onslaught of clever and often hilarious ads. Awards, even television specials sprung up to highlight the most outlandish and memorable advertisements of the year. Who will ever forget Clara Peller's delivery of her famous line, "Where's the beef?"

While awards like the Clio recognized highly creative and often remarkably funny ads, they masked the very serious problem advertisers were having getting their sales messages across to the public.

Unfortunately for marketers, what is new and creative to consumers one day becomes expected and mundane the next. So as time went on, agencies found the need to push the boundaries of creativity further and further, often at the expense of crowding out the sales message. Super Bowl ads are a shining example of just how detached ads have become from salesmanship. While they are highly entertaining, they are also the equivalent of dressing your best salesman in clown shoes and a Speedo. The level of entertainment needed to break through to consumers is so high it over-shadows the purpose for the ad. The end result is that people remember the ad but have no idea what product it was promoting.

Getting people's attention takes time away from selling. Because advertisements by their nature are short, anything that cuts into precious selling time can cripple or even kill an ad's ability to produce sales.

If that's not enough, things have gotten much worse for marketers. Consumers are now proactively fighting against promotional messages. They have enlisted politicians to create laws that forbid companies from calling, faxing or emailing them. They have armed themselves with devices that block sales messages such as TiVo and spam filters, and have tripled the number of preset dials on their car radios. In addition, they can now subscribe to commercial-free satellite radio. It just keeps getting more difficult to reach consumers.

Even the powerful and ubiquitous advertising industry has declined as promotional dollars flow into new promotional directions like the Internet and custom publishing.

Although advertising is having its share of difficulties today, it had a powerful beginning.

During the period from about 1870 to 1970, advertising was one of four important elements that converged to form our consumer society. Those elements: industry, advertising, the media and the public, worked together over time, building on one another, with each becoming larger and more powerful with the passing of time.

Here's how the upward spiral worked. Businesses

created products and hired advertising agencies to promote them. Advertising agencies purchased space in media outlets to run their ads. The media delivered the ads to the public, and the public bought the products. As people bought more products, it provided more revenue for the businesses, which in turn created more products that, of course, required more ads. The increased ad purchases meant more revenues for the media who brought more ads to the consumers, who purchased even more products.

On and on the spiral continued until it eventually created multinational companies like Proctor & Gamble and General Electric, major brands like Coca-Cola and Kleenex, powerhouse ad agencies like Foote Cone & Belding, and Ogilvy & Mather, media giants like Time Warner and Rupert Murdoch's News Corporation, and of course a consumer society the likes of which the world had never seen.

You can't overestimate the strength of the promotional infrastructure created during this time.

If you were fortunate enough to have created an established brand during this time, advertising has remained a powerful, although expensive, way to reach and remind consumers to purchase. Advertising is also still used effectively for products, such as an inexpensive wristwatch, that satisfy pent-up consumer demands and can be explained in a matter of seconds.

However, if you have a complex product, or are trying to introduce a new product, brief ads don't work very well. Introducing new and complex products takes salesmanship, and as we've pointed out, the need for creativity hasn't left much room for salesmanship in the predominant promotional channel: advertising.

So how do you introduce salesmanship back into your marketing?

The first step is to change your mindset about advertising. Realize that in today's world advertising works well for reminding people to purchase but not very well for selling new and complex products. Remember that advertising is just a vehicle that carries a message, and that message can be easily moved to other "non-advertising" vehicles that are better suited to a longer, more persuasive message.

The next step is to reacquaint yourself with the promotional process. To put effective selling tactics back in your marketing you need to understand the promotional process so you can build effective, teaching sales messages.

The third step is to identify promotional channels that will both accommodate a complete sales message and be embraced by consumers.

The following chapters will give you the basics for understanding the fundamentals of marketing and promotion, show you how to create sales messages that resonate with consumers, and help you identify promotional channels that work well for teaching consumers to purchase your products.

Chapter Two

Building the foundation for your promotional thinking

———————————————

To better understand our business, Kocina Marketing Companies, I teach a college marketing class. By the end of the semester every student knows the four Ps of marketing. It's elementary. Yet in thirty years of business I've found only a handful of people who remember them.

Before you read further, do you know the four Ps of marketing? You should.

The four Ps of marketing are Product, Price, Place and Promotion.

If you have worked in marketing for a while, it may seem simplistic to re-learning the four Ps of marketing, but words are a tool the mind uses to group and organize concepts, and to understand marketing clearly, you'll need to know the terms for these concepts. As you commit these and other terms used in this short book to memory, you will be pleasantly surprised at the way they will shape your thinking. It's like adding horsepower to your brain.

The following are brief definitions of Marketing and its four Ps. Get to know them. When you are ready, take out a piece of paper and test yourself.

Marketing: *The action of planning and executing product development, pricing, distribution and promotion for the purpose of satisfying both the needs of the organization and the individual.*

This definition of marketing cuts a wide swath. See if you can name an area of a company that marketing, as defined here, wouldn't include. People who are truly the "head of marketing" are high up the ladder.

Product: *An item, either tangible or a service, which is produced for sale.*

Note that for the purpose of marketing there is no distinction between a physical product and a service. The term product covers both.

Price: *That which is given up in exchange for a product.*

Money is not the only price that people pay for their products. To get tickets to an event that is sure to sell out, attendees may have to stand in line long before the tickets go on sale. The time spent in line is also a price that is paid for the ticket.

Place *(Distribution): The chain of physical locations where both raw materials and finished products reside and the processes involved in bringing them to the consumer.*

Distribution is a better word than place, but three

Ps and a D wouldn't be as catchy.

Sometimes promotional events happen in the distribution channel. A manufacturer might offer a broker the authority to discount a product if a retailer is willing to offer the product "on sale".

Promotion: *The communication of a product's features, benefits and desire satisfaction, for the purpose of influencing a purchase.*

The term Promotion has multiple meanings in marketing depending on how it is used. In the context of the four Ps, that is how it's defined.

Most of a marketer's work is done in the areas of Promotion and Place. It takes a lot of ongoing work to promote products and to develop and maintain distribution channels.

There is much less time spent on the other two Ps, Product and Price, and most of that work happens in the early stages of the product's lifecycle. R&D takes care of creating the Product and some blend of management and accounting determine a profitable Price. There is additional work done on both Product and Price throughout the product's life but not at the level of the early stages. Once a product makes its way to the marketplace, it is usually just a matter of keeping the Product current by making minor improvements, and adjusting the Price for maximum profit or promotional discounts.

Marketing encompasses a big piece of what goes on in a company so it's complex and difficult, and that's normal. What's abnormal is when marketing gets confusing. Categorizing marketing into the four Ps is the first step to bringing your work and everything that flows from it into focus.

Unfortunately, as with many of the words in the English language, some terms in marketing have more than one meaning. There are two words to look out for. One is marketing and the other is promotion. Not only do these words have multiple meanings, sometimes people use them out of context. For instance, the word promotion has a different meaning when used to describe the Promotion P than it does when referring to promotion as a category of the promotional mix (which we will cover later).

Marketing is commonly misused in place of the word promotion. Someone might say, "I handle all the marketing for product X" when in fact they have nothing to do with R&D and no control over pricing. They are actually in charge of Promotion. Or someone will tell you they are writing a marketing letter when if fact they are writing a promotional letter.

You might think I'm just playing with semantics but if you want to think clearly about marketing it's important to use the right terms to keep your thoughts in order. The four Ps are the components of marketing under which all the other elements are subsumed. Knowing them is the first step in making marketing organized and understandable.

Chapter Three

Understanding the promotional implications of the product lifecycle stages

---

In order to develop the right promotional building blocks and select the appropriate promotional channels for salesmanship, you need to know what stage of the Product Lifecycle the product is in. All products have a lifecycle. The lifecycle is broken up into four stages. They are: 1) The Introductory Stage, 2) The Growth Stage, 3) The Mature Stage, and 4) The Decline Stage.

The introductory and growth stages are where brands are created. The mature and decline stages are where brands are maintained. Determining the stage of the lifecycle helps identify the promotional channels that will work best to promote the product.

During the first two stages, introductory and growth, consumers are unfamiliar with the features and benefits of the product and how the product will serve their needs. Not only are new products unfamiliar to consumers, today many products are quite complex and require an in-depth explanation. Consumers need to be taught about emerging products. During the first two lifecycle stages, the promotional objective is to reach out to consumers and teach them to buy. Only certain promotional channels offer the opportunity to teach.

Teaching consumers about a product requires two important elements. The first and most critical is that the consumer is willing to listen. It's difficult to teach someone who isn't paying attention. Unfortunately, today's consumers not only ignore sales messages, they actively block them. What they can't block they simply ignore. So, when introducing a product to the market, it's important to find promotional channels where consumers willingly listen.

Even though consumers are becoming increasingly resistant to sales messages, there are still plenty of promotional channels where people pay attention. Later, in chapter eight, you will find a comprehensive list of promotional channels (where people still listen) that work well for teaching.

The second element needed for "teaching" consumers is an appropriate educational message. Because advertising has conditioned marketers to pare down the message to fit the space and lower the cost, it can be a challenge to think about products as full stories worthy of someone's time.

After the product moves into the mature and decline stages, the need to teach about the product goes away. Everybody knows what the product is and what it does. Normally if a product makes it to this stage it has become a cash cow. The challenge during these two stages is to remind consumers to buy the product in order to maintain market share. Reminding consumers to repurchase can be expensive and is often done primarily through advertising channels.

Chapter Four

Zero in on a market segmentation strategy

A product's market is anyone who has or may one day have the need for the product and has the ability to make or influence the purchase. Markets can be divided into submarkets based on similarities such as demographics, geography, psychographics, etc. Most markets can be organized into many submarkets.

The fact that markets can be divided up into submarkets is one of the reasons promotion gets confusing. Each submarket when viewed by itself can look like a gold mine. That's why it's important to have a market segmentation strategy to help you stay on track.

There are four strategies to choose from:

1) undifferentiated
2) concentrated
3) multi-segmented
4) micro-segmented

Using an undifferentiated strategy, everyone within the market receives the same promotional message. Using a concentrated strategy, a promotional message is tailored to the most lucrative submarket. And with the multi-segmented and micro-segmented approach, unique promotional messages are developed for two or more submarkets.

Each strategy has advantages and disadvantages. Using the undifferentiated strategy and the concentrated strategy are the least expensive and the least work. These strategies require only one message so there is no effort expended creating unique promotions for each submarket.

It is possible that more profit might be gained using a concentrated strategy over an undifferentiated strategy because tailoring the message specifically to a highly motivated, actively seeking subgroup could be more productive than a general message sent to a broader market.

Multi-segmented and micro-segmented strategies will net the largest market share but they require more work and more money because multiple messages need to be created and delivered.

****

When products are in the introductory stage of the product lifecycle, revenues are low. Because of budget restrictions most companies, even Fortune 500 companies introducing new products, start out using an undifferentiated or concentrated strategy. As the product moves into the growth stage and sales generate sufficient revenue to support the added expense, promotions normally evolve to a multi-segmented or even micro-segmented strategies in order to capture a larger share of the market.

The danger of adopting a multi-segmented market strategy too early in the product's lifecycle is that both marketing dollars and human resources are spread too thin. In the early stages of promoting a product, opportunities abound and it can be difficult to say no to some of them. Going off in too many directions is a common mistake when introducing a new product. It's like the monkey that has its arms full of bananas but just can't resist reaching for one more. As he picks up one, he drops three.

Knowing the limits of your promotional budget and human resources, selecting a market segmentation strategy that fits, and being disciplined enough to say no to opportunities that fall outside these boundaries is key to developing a successful promotional strategy.

Chapter Five

Pinpoint your customers' desires

The best promotional messages strike a chord with the consumer. They resonate in harmony with the way people feel in their heart of hearts. Once a connection is made at that level, the consumer is more likely to buy. To reach the consumer on an emotional level, the promotion needs to communicate feelings more than features and benefits. Features and benefits are facts, and consumers' actions spring from emotions, not facts.

If human action was driven by facts we would all eat the correct number of calories each day, exercise regularly, drive cars based on safety ratings and start saving for retirement at a young age to take advantage of compound interest. Instead we eat fast food, watch on average three hours of TV a day, buy sporty cars, and create expensive life-styles that stifle our ability to save.

Focusing promotions on features and benefits is a mistake. It's fine to include them, but realize they are not the hot buttons that cause consumers to buy. It's desire that causes consumers to act.

Tune into your feelings and use them as a gauge when you read the following three definitions. You'll note that there are no feelings associated with the word features, some feelings associated with benefits and that desire is all about feelings.

Now take a moment, become aware of your feelings and read the following definitions.
Feature: a distinctive attribute or aspect
Benefit: an advantage gained from something
Desire: a strong feeling of wanting something or wishing for something to happen

The feeling of desire stems from an internal im-balance. It's the need to move away from the way things are and toward the way we believe they should be.

To assure promotions play to desires, marketers should create a list of reasons the market or submarket desires their product and prioritize them. The list should be used when creating promotions and then used again as a benchmark to evaluate the promotion once it is finished.

Feelings can be difficult to put into words. It takes more language to express desires than it does features and benefits. It also takes more effort to identify them. So plan on spending some time, maybe even weeks or months, as you work on defining why consumers desire your product. Good sales professionals know how to artfully tap into people's desires.

Keep in mind that different submarkets will desire the same product for different reasons. The desires for a haircut differ vastly between parents and their teen. There may be some shared desires such as the desire to spend as little as possible but there is a reason submarkets are submarkets and that's because they share unique desires exclusive to their group.

****

Most new and complex products require substantial explanation. Yet, if you don't quickly make a connection to the audience's desires, you will lose them and in the process lose the sale. Knowing your customers' key desires and getting to them quickly is imperative. If you are able to make a connection with consumers' desires right out of the gate, they will take more time to listen. And the more time you have to teach them about your product, the more likely the consumers will be to buy. Understanding your customers' desires and building upon them is good salesmanship.

Chapter Six

Develop a positioning statement as an essential ingredient and measurement tool

---

A positioning statement documents how a product is positioned in the mind of the consumer. It is the essence of the consumer's need for the product. How a product is positioned will affect the makeup of the marketing mix. For instance, if a positioning statement stresses high value, consideration will need to be made to establishing a price that meets the expectation of the consumer. If the positioning statement claims fast delivery, there will have to be special attention paid to distribution channels (the place P).

Positioning statements are brief and comprised of features, benefits, and most importantly, the consumer's desire for a product. They consist of plain language woven together to form the nucleus of what you want the consumer to understand about your product. Think of positioning statements as code that will be included in all your promotional efforts.

If consumers decode your promotional messages correctly, and you were to overhear them telling a friend about your product, you would find that they explained the essence of your product exactly right.

There are a variety of variables to consider when creating a positioning statement including price, product usage, customer type, product category, value, etc. A product's positioning statement may focus on only one or two variables, or it may contain many. There is no perfect model for creating a positioning statement because all positioning statements are unique. One good model for getting started is: to (target segment and desire) is (concept) that (point to that difference).[1]Note that if you choose a multi-segmented marketing approach, you will need a unique positioning statement for each submarket.

It's much easier to explain what a positioning statement is, than to create one. The saying "I would have written you a shorter letter but I didn't have the time" points out the effort that is needed to distill thoughts down to a clear, concise message. It takes work. You may have to anguish over many drafts before you are satisfied.

As a positioning statement is developed it may cause marketers to reevaluate the priority of features, benefits and customer desires. And as with all the building blocks of promotions, it will need to be modified as the marketing climate changes. It's not uncommon for circumstances to change so dramatically over time that the products need to be modified and substantially repositioned in the consumer's mind. Most fast food restaurants are transitioning from being viewed as burger joints to convenient locations that offer healthy food choices for people on the go.

1 *Principles of Marketing*. Philip Kotler, Gary Armstrong 12e P.210

Developing a positioning statement has three main benefits. First, it helps the marketing team understand clearly the message it is trying to convey through its promotions. Second, it acts as a basis for creating promotions. And third, it can be used as a measurement to ensure promotions contain the messages they are supposed to.

Chapter Seven

Establish your intended results

The most important part of promotions is the results they deliver. Sometimes it's a direct sale and other times it can be driving people to retail locations or collecting e-mail addresses. Whatever the intention, results are the reason for the promotion.

Because it's easy for marketing teams to get sidetracked as promotions develop, starting with the end in mind by creating a list of intended results will help keep everyone on course.

It is also a good idea to write the copy for the results portion of the promotion first. It is hard work creating promotions and everyone does their best work in the beginning when they are fresh. It makes sense to work on the most important part of the promotion, the intended results, when people have the most energy.

Here is a list of some common intended results.
1. Solicit a direct purchase
2. Harvest personal data such as e-mails, phone numbers and addresses
3. Prompt consumers to make contact with the company
4. Generate sales leads
5. Set the stage for a personal sales call
6. Drive consumers to retail locations
7. Educate and inform
8. Drive traffic to a Web site
9. Build a reputation
10. Get your contact information into their records

Chapter Eight

Define the promotional mix

To this point you should:

1. Know the four Ps of marketing: product, place, price and promotion
2. Understand why it's important to know what stage of the product lifecycle your product is in.
3. Understand the different market segmentation strategies: undifferentiated, concentrated, multi-segmented, and micro-segmented.
4. Know what a market is and how it can be divided into submarkets.
5. Realize the subtle but important differences between features, benefits, and consumer desires.
6. Understand the importance of creating a positioning statement and know how to use it.

7. And finally, realize the importance of creating a list of desired results and why you should work on this at the beginning of the project.

It is now time to discuss creating promotional messages and pushing them out through the individual promotional channels. These channels are grouped into broad categories called the Promotional Mix.

Traditionally the promotional mix grouped all promotional channels into four categories: public relations, advertising, personal selling, and promotions. Recently two methods of promotion have grown to become their own categories, the Internet, and custom publishing and broadcasting. All promotions fit into one of these six categories.

The categories of the promotional mix, except for promotions, are self-defining. (Note that the word promotions has a slightly different meaning here than the promotion P in the marketing mix.) The category of promotions is not as easy to understand as the others. It includes things like loyalty programs, sampling, cross product promotions, etc. It also includes arrangements to promote the product within the distribution channels such as special pricing arrangements made with suppliers, brokers, wholesalers, etc. As an example, a company might offer a retailer a fifty-cent per case discount provided they put up an in-store display. This would fall under the promotional mix category of promotions. Promotions usually call upon consumers to take an action as is the case with coupons and loyalty programs.

The best way to understand the promotional mix category "promotions" is to think of it as everything that the other five categories are not. If you can't put it into one of the other categories (public relations, advertising, personal selling, Internet, custom publishing and broadcasting) then it goes in promotions.

You might ask, why is it important to categorize the individual promotional channels into the broad categories of the promotional mix? Like markets and submarkets, each category of the promotional mix has characteristics that are unique to that group. The makeup of the promotional mix will change depending on the needs of the marketer.

Some characteristics of the elements of the promotional mix are price, audience size, frequency of the message, and the opportunity to deliver a long or short message.

A company with an established brand that wants to maintain market share, and has substantial resources, will have a promotional mix that is heavy in advertising. A company that is introducing a new product, or has a complex product, and has a limited budget, will likely have a promotional mix that will rely heavily on public relations.

Chapter Nine

Understand individual promotional channels and categorize them by REACH & TEACH and REACH & TOUCH

To this point we have dealt with the process of defining who the market is and how to prepare the base elements of the message they will receive. Now it's time to identify the opportunities to distribute the message. Stemming from each category of the promotional mix are individual Promotional Channels. The promotional channels are where the message passes through and into the minds of consumers. For example, each individual salesperson is a unique promotional channel that stems from the personal sales category of the promotional mix. Each advertisement and direct mail piece is a promotional channel that stems from advertising. And all story content in newspapers, magazines, radio and TV programs are promotional channels of public relations. As you move the ingredients of your message through the promotional mix and out into the individual promotional channels, you will see that the individual promotional channels can be divided into two categories; those that allow you the time and space to fully develop your message, and those that don't.

Some promotional channels are "wide" and have more room for salesmanship, and consequently work better for teaching consumers about new and complex products. We have termed these wide channels REACH & TEACH promotional channels.

Other promotional channels are "narrow" and offer the opportunity for brief communication. We have termed these narrow channels REACH & TOUCH promotional channels because there isn't enough time to do any real teaching. REACH & TOUCH channels offer little more than an opportunity to tap the consumer on the shoulder and mention the product.

Radio and television commercials are an example of narrow promotional channels. With only thirty to sixty seconds to deliver the sales message, the communication is brief.

Most advertisers consider both reach (the volume of people who will receive the message) and frequency (the number of times an individual will receive the message) when planning their campaigns. The need for frequency stems from the fact that consumers need to see or hear an ad many times before the message finally registers with them.

With REACH & TOUCH promotional channels, frequency is necessary. With wide REACH & TEACH promotional channels, such as an article in a magazine, the ability to communicate a complete sales message makes frequency much less important and often unnecessary.

The majority of REACH & TOUCH promotions are ads produced by large corporations for the purpose of supporting their existing brands. Revenues derived from these "cash cow" brands fund the massive advertising campaigns needed to maintain, grow or recapture market share. Although it is expensive, advertising offers the unique opportunity to touch consumers with un-limited frequency.

In some instances advertising channels can also be used to introduce a product to the market. Advertising works to introduce products that need little explanation, can be fully understood in a matter of seconds, have a substantial latent de-mand, and profit margins sufficient to cover the advertising expense.

Most new products however, require lengthy ex-planations.

The marketing channels that facilitate an expanded explanation of the product—REACH & TEACH promotional channels, are the channels that offer you the opportunity to use salesmanship.

There are three main reasons products are promoted using REACH & TEACH promotional channels: the product is brand-new so consumers are unaware of it, the product is complex and difficult to understand, and the product is new to the market or submarket i.e. the benefits of an AARP membership to someone turning fifty.

Promotional channels best suited for REACHING and TEACHING consumers are found primarily within the promotional mix categories of public relations, personal selling, custom publishing and the Internet. The media is the biggest. The public may tune out the commercials but they love their stories. Convincing reporters and producers to do product stories is a powerful and far-reaching promotional force. It's a great way to introduce salesmanship into your promotional mix. The Internet is another place where people are actively listening. Events and expos are also good places to explain new and complex products. In addition you can find a few good REACH & TEACH promotional channels in advertising and promotion, such as direct mail and symposium lectures.

The following is a list of the six promotional mix categories and many of the promotional channels that stem from them. The promotional channels that lend themselves best to REACHING and TEACHING are underlined and in italics.

PROMOTIONAL CHANNELS

Personal Selling
Face to Face
Telephone
Word of Mouth

Advertising
National Newspaper
Local Newspaper
National Magazine
Local Magazine

National Television
Local Television
National Radio
Local Radio
Internet
Trade/Professional
Alternative
Collateral Materials
Yellow Pages
Direct Mail
Indoor Advertising
Outdoor Advertising
Logo Placement

Public Relations
National Newspaper
Local Newspaper
National Magazine
Local Magazine
National Television
Local Television
National Radio
Local Radio
Internet

Trade/Professional
Press Kit
Press Release
Speaking Engagements
Events
Lectures
Celebrity Endorsements
Spokespeople
Sponsorships
Product Placements
Charitable Affiliations

Custom Publishing
Magazine
Newsletter
Audio Podcast
Video Podcast
Book
E-Newsletter

Internet
Direct Sales
Education

Data Collection
Lead Collection
Ads
Links
Blogs
Surveys
Sales Support
Webinars
RSS Feeds
Search Engine Rank

Promotions
Coupons
Premiums
Contests
Sweepstakes
Sampling
Point of Purchase Promotions
Loyalty Programs
Premiums
Cross Promotions
Loyalty Programs

PLACE (Distribution)

Vendors
Suppliers
Agents
Brokers
Wholesalers
Retailers

When selecting REACH & TEACH promotional channels there are a couple things to keep in mind. The first is to determine if the audience is actively listening. Even if there are no restrictions that prevent the delivery of a complete sales message, it doesn't guarantee that the audience is listening. Direct mail is a good example. A substantial percentage of direct mail pieces are thrown in the trash without ever being read.

Another variable to consider is the size of the audience. Contrast an article on the front page of the lifestyle section of a major newspaper with a podcast available on an obscure Web site.

Media news stories are a powerful promotional channel with extraordinary ability to REACH & TEACH the masses. People may tune out the ads but they actively listen to the stories. And the audience sizes, even with minor publications and broadcasts are quite large.

Another advantage news articles and show appearances offer is that the media industry is filled with talented communicators. Some of them will be able explain why people should use your product better than you can. They are in tune with their audience and can help draw out and emphasize the things that are most important to them.

The role public relations plays as it pertains to product promotion will be discussed in more detail later.

Chapter Ten

Counter the nudging effect

Promotional channels are where the fine focus tactics and task work are done. There are countless details involved in creating a single promotion. Take for instance everything you would need to consider if you were planning a promotional event. What is the purpose of the event? What topics should the speakers address? How big should the room be? Should there be food, maybe dinner? How about dessert? What's the budget? How will it be promoted? On and on the questions go.

Executing promotions, whether a speaking engagement or an ad in a trade publication, can be an enormous amount of work. Because there are so many fine focus tactics and tasks involved with promotions, it's easy to get lost in the details. The consequence of this is that the details have a nudging effect. As one small detail leads to another and then another, it can take you in directions you didn't intend.

There is no escaping the many detailed tasks required to accomplish each promotional effort. The only counter measure is to have a firm grasp of the marketing process. Someone who understands marketing academically will know where the details fit within the framework. Keeping promotions on track saves money, time and produces better results.

The more firmly you have the terms and processes of promotion established in your mind, the more likely you will be to create individual promotions that stay on target with your goals.

Chapter Eleven

Creating content chains

Once you have created a promotion and pushed it out through a promotional channel, that promotional content can be used as a basis for creating other promotions in other promotional channels. For example, let's say an organization's top salesperson has developed an effective voice mail message they use when they call someone for the first time. It's brief, to the point and has an interesting twist that gets people calling back. It's possible that the voice mail message could also be used as a concept for a postcard mailing. It could also be documented and distributed to other salespeople for their use, and in addition it could be turned into a 30 second radio commercial.

Another example is using a television interview as the basis for an article in a promotional newsletter. The television interview could also be high-lighted on the company Web site or it could be referenced on a sell sheet used by the field sales staff.

The process of stringing promotions together like this is called building a Content Chain.

Carefully following the promotional process for creating messages and then stringing them together to form content chains will create integrated marketing. No matter what the consumer's contact point, be it the salesperson, the Web site or a direct mail piece, they will receive a noticeably consistent and sales-rich promotional message.

Chapter Twelve

Harnessing creativity

There is both a science and an art to marketing. The science is breaking down marketing into understandable elements such as the marketing mix, the four phases of a product lifecycle, markets and submarkets, etc. The art is pulling all the elements together into communication that influences the consumer's desire to purchase.

There is so much talk of creativity in marketing and especially promotions that it makes sense to discuss its place in promotions.

Creativity can be categorized in two ways: creativity that comes from working within boundaries and creativity that comes from having no boundaries. Creativity without boundaries may be valued in the art world, but it doesn't have much use in promotions. Here is an example of creativity without boundaries; Bill cuts his pen into little pieces and makes earrings out of them and gives them to every 37th woman he meets unless it happens to be Tuesday in which case he gives her a 1956 buffalo nickel he has bent at a 93 degree angle and spray painted blue. When you take away boundaries from creativity you end up with gibberish.

Creativity with boundaries is creativity that is used to achieve a result. It's really nothing more than using your mind to come up with ideas that are beyond the most obvious. On the surface it might seem as though restrictions would stifle creativity but they don't. It's actually the opposite. It takes creativity to surmount the restrictions.

Some people's minds naturally find unconventional ways to connect the dots. Others limit their thinking to the most obvious ideas. Drawing out creativity is a simple process anyone can learn. It's only a matter of identifying the problem, writing down the most obvious ideas for solving it, setting them aside, and then thinking of some others.

Here are two simple tools that can be used to make anyone seem creatively gifted.

Start by drawing a circle in the middle of a page and write the problem you would like to solve inside that circle. For instance, the challenge could be to create a direct mail piece that will be opened and read by every person who receives it. Next draw ten additional circles outside the center circle. Now put your mind to work coming up with ways to solve the problem. Each time you think of a new idea, write it in one of the circles. Don't stop until you have filled all ten circles.

The first few circles filled will contain the most obvious ideas. Once you have those out of the way, other less obvious ideas will follow. Practice this for a while and ideas will come quickly.

Another way to draw out creativity is to pick ten random words from a dictionary and use them to spur thinking about your problem. For example, let's say you are exhibiting at an upcoming expo and you want to find a way to increase the number of leads you will get. Ten random words are forgone, inhaler, mainstay, mystic, polar, salute, staple, Texan, thaw, and unload.

The word inhaler might spark the idea of using the aroma of food to draw more people to the booth. The word mystic could bring to mind hiring a palm reader as a draw. Salute could conjure up the image of a highly visual exhibit space filled with flags and banners. Random words can uncover some useful ideas.

Be careful not to rely too heavily on creativity. Creativity is a good tool to help with promotions but it's no substitute for following a well thought out process. Remember Edison's famous quote, "Genius is one percent inspiration and ninety-nine percent perspiration."

A person of average creative ability can develop successful promotional programs if they understand marketing principles, follow the process, think a little, and do the work.

Chapter Thirteen

Take control of the most powerful promotional channels: the media

---

Public relations is the icing on the cake when it comes to REACH & TEACH product promotion. Not much will outsell a well-written article or broadcast. Most of the reasons media stories sell so well are obvious; they offer the opportunity to tell a complete story, there is an implied third party endorsement by the media outlet, media stories are our primary source for finding out what's going on in our communities and around the world, etc.

But here is a reason that might surprise you; people are in a state of hypnosis when they watch TV or read a story.

It can put people on edge when I tell them they have been hypnotized by the media. Some people think it sounds far-fetched. Others think I'm probably making something out of nothing. The common thread is that they find it hard to believe there is a mysterious force manipulating their thinking as they watch TV.

But consider this; during hypnosis the human brain operates in the alpha state of consciousness which is eight to thirteen cycles per second as measured by an EEG. This is the same stage of consciousness we drift through as we pass from being alert (the beta state) to falling asleep (the theta and delta states). It's also the state we slip into when we are watching TV, reading newspaper and magazines, or listening to the radio. Throughout the day everyone slips in and out of the alpha state of consciousness.

During the alpha state our mental guard is down and we are more apt to believe things without questioning them. That's why hypnotists can help people lose weight or stop smoking. It's also why you can enjoy a Superman movie without questioning why an actor in a blue leotard and red cape can fly.

You might think that after the movie or a sitcom you become alert and realize it was just make-believe. Tell that to an actor who has had their career crippled because they have been typecast. Even though we know intellectually that the actor is not the person they play, on some level we believe they are. The same goes with reading a fiction book. We know it's not real but on some level we have memories that seem real.

With fiction, there is an obvious contrast with reality that allows us to see the silliness of what we have been persuaded to believe. Take for instance the way many older people feel about John Wayne, affectionately known as "The Duke." His legacy is that of a rough and tumble, no nonsense western hero.

The truth, as most people know, is that John Wayne's real name was Marion Morrison. And Marion, the actor who grew up in Iowa, did something that most of us would find embarrassing. As an adult, Marion dressed up in a cowboy costume and pretended to shoot bad guys.

It's an amusing example but it points out the almost supernatural ability of the media to shape the opinion of the masses. It's evident that under the right conditions people can be persuaded to have feelings that under normal circumstances they would question or even reject.

Teaching the masses about a product when they are in an alpha state of consciousness is a good way to get your message across and see that it sticks. I believe it's the most effective way to brand a product. It's also the least expensive.

You'd think given the selling power of the media that it would be a fully developed promotional channel. Instead, for all practical purposes it's untapped.

Surprisingly it's the PR industry that has kept PR from blossoming into the powerful promotional force it can be.

Thanks largely to Edward Bernays, who is considered the father of PR, people in the industry are conditioned to see themselves as counselors and practitioners, not salespeople. A quick look at the PRSA's (Public Relations Society of America) Web site will give you a sense of the industry's highbrow attitude. Many come into the field with journalism backgrounds and they tend to be liberal leaning.

Marketers are often frustrated with PR firms. In truth they shouldn't be. The reason they are frustrated is they want PR firms to be something they are not. As counselors and practitioners, public relations professionals do their best work mediating between a company and the many "publics" they deal with.

Most public relations work is done in the areas of investor relations, community relations, crisis management, event planning, employee relations, etc.

I think it's safe to say that most PR professionals would not consider themselves dyed-in-the-wool capitalists. Putting a traditional public relations firm in charge of selling is like putting a rifle in the hands of a medic. It's a mismatch of ideals. Traditional PR firms are not organizations meant to drive sales and they never will be.

The PR industry's billing model of hourly charges and monthly retainers doesn't sit well with marketers either. For a marketer who is under pressure to produce sales, paying a PR firm and not knowing what, if anything, they will get for their money irks them. They are used to the advertising model of pay for an ad, get an ad.

So even though PR firms have access to the most powerful promotional channel, they don't sell many stories that promote products. For most of them, it's simply not in their nature.

If you want to exploit PR as a promotional channel and mobilize reporters into a national sales force, you'll need to do it yourself or hire a hybrid firm like ours to help you.

Note:

Marketing is a complex process with many moving parts. For visual learners I have created a poster that outlines key steps in the process. It was originally included with this book. If you are reading this book and don't have the poster, you can order one by going to our website, publicity.com. At publicity.com you will also find content that will be useful in planning and executing a REACH & TEACH promotional strategy.